Short Stories

from the

Long Links

a collection of golf related tales

Richard E. Todd

Follow The Golf Rules at…

www. TheGolfRules .com

DEDICATION

To every golfer,
regardless of handicap, age, or frequency of play;
who, when not playing the game,
enjoys watching it, talking about it,
dreaming about it, or reading related stories.

To the latter, here are my tales for your enjoyment.

INTRODUCTION

Short Stories from the Long Links is a collection of tales about the ancient game of golf.

Some of these stories are inspired from real life events, daily activities, and golf endeavors as relayed to the author. If you have a unique or inspiring golf story, please submit it to The Golf Rules. Your tale might be included in a future publishing.

For more golf-related books and stories, links to follow me on Facebook, Twitter, WordPress, and YouTube, and to learn more about the author and upcoming and past events, visit **www.TheGolfRules.com**.

STORIES

The Early Bird

AFTER DINNER, while at the club, Rodger overheard a couple of members arguing about tee times.

"I much prefer the late afternoon to tee off," one club member said. "The day is starting to wind down and it makes for a more relaxed round. And if your golf is timed properly, you can finish at the precise moment that dinner is set."

"I'm sorry to disagree, but you have it all wrong," another member stated. "The absolute best time to tee off is first thing in the morning. I don't mean to say you should be one of the first couple of groups to tee off but, rather, I mean be *the* first person to play, before the course has been touched by a single soul. There is an energy in the air. Some in the Far East say it has to do with solar flares or something cosmic as the Earth itself begins to wake up. Codswallop, if you ask me, but there is a difference in attitude while playing that early in the day."

"Yes, I agree. It's called lack of sleep," the first responded.

"To look out over the many fairways, still wet from the morning dew without a single footprint on them is something beautiful to observe. I've also found that it improves my game!"

At that last comment Rodger perked up. He was always looking for ways to decrease his handicap and had been unable to move it more than a fraction of a stroke in a very long time.

"You're joking," the first member said to the second.

"I am not. The last time I played first for the day I hit more fairways and made more putts. It was as if I couldn't miss, like my ball was a groundhog running from its shadow to his den, which was in the bottom of the cup."

At this point, Rodger could be seen staring at a nearby plant, with his glass halfway to his lips, motionless for the longest time. Had someone paid any attention to him, they surely would have thought him to have had a stroke.

"But I like my evening rounds, and the mornings come too early for me. With that, I will gladly give up a few strokes for a good night's sleep," the first said as both chuckled and moved towards the parlor.

Still in a catatonic state, Rodger began to calculate how he could start his rounds earlier. This idea was all he could think about throughout the night.

The next day, Rodger rang the pro shop at a second past opening.

"Good morning. Can I arrange a tee time for you?" the voice on the phone asked.

"Yes," said Rodger. "What is your earliest availability tomorrow morning?"

"Our first opening is nine forty-five."

"That won't do at all. How about the next day?"

"We have a nine o'clock opening."

"That's still too late. What is the earliest time you allow someone to tee off?"

"That would be eight o'clock, sir."

"When do you have an eight o'clock tee time vacant?"

"Next Thursday."

"I'll take it," Rodger stated and hung up the phone.

~

For over a week, Rodger dreamed of that early morning round and of dropping a stroke, maybe three, from his total.

Finally, the day came. He checked in at the clubhouse with haste and hurried off, driver in hand. Upon arrival at the first tee, anticipating that glorious untouched Eden, he stopped on the first tee box and surveyed the fairway. Footprints were seen all around the teeing area and down the fairway. Barely visible were trails on the putting green.

"Drat," Rodger said. "Some scoundrel played earlier. Well, I may as well golf some as I'm here."

And so he did. Playing in a foul mood, he scored one over his handicap.

"Absurd," he said to himself after adding his scorecard on the 18th.

Storming into the clubhouse he asked when the next first tee time of the day was available.

"Next Friday, sir," the attendant replied.

"No, no, no, no, no, no. I must tee off early," he exclaimed. Then, he was awed by an idea that formed in his head, like a ball hit with a wedge from off the green, landing on the putting surface before rattling the flagstick. "Can I tee off *before* the first tee time?" he inquired hesitantly.

"No, sir," the attendant replied with a confused look on his face. "That's why they call it the first tee time."

Rodger then slowly slid a hundred-dollar bill onto the desk and gave a sly smile.

"Oh, I see. Hmmm. Yes," he said with a pause. "Let me know, personally, what time you would like to tee off and I will make the proper arrangements with the staff."

"Excellent," Rodger said, then thought for a moment. *I don't want anyone to see me teeing off before the start. Thirty minutes should do the trick.* "Seven thirty, my good man," he said, then half skipped out the door.

That evening over dinner, Rodger quietly planned his attack while enjoying some perfectly prepared pheasant. "I'll need time to wake, have breakfast, get to the course, and warm up a tad. Hmm. I'll need to get up about half past five. That's manageable. Good, I'm all set."

The next morning, after everything that needed done was, he arrived at the tee box. His anxious heart dropped. Footprints. They were everywhere.

"How can this be? Unless someone else is trying the same play as I am. Well, I'll show them," he said to himself as he began his round.

After finishing, Rodger tallied the scores while on the veranda of the clubhouse. "Over again. At this rate I'll be adding two to my handicap by the end of the month."

"Seven fifteen, Wednesday," he whispered to the clerk as he walked through the pro shop.

The rest of that day, Rodger barely worked as he reviewed his calendar to see how he could arrange his meetings with clients so that there would be enough time to sleep, eat and, of course, play golf.

That evening, he calculated the alarm must wake him by five o'clock to accomplish his task of arriving at the course for the next early tee time.

Groggily, he arose the next morning and went through his daily constitutionals. He was tired but prepared for a magical round of golf. His spirits lifted as he headed to the first tee, but then they crumbled as he was met with the same footprints throughout the green grass.

"Seven o'clock, tomorrow," was all he said to the attendant after finishing his round.

Again and again, he tried to start his round before the sacred ground had been touched. And over and over he was disappointed.

For several weeks, Rodger juggled his schedule to fit in more golf. He would come in late for work, if at all. He would eat dinner at three o'clock in the afternoon, and go to bed very early, sometimes while the sun was shining. All this was done so that he could be the first person to play the course.

But day in and day out, as he approached the first tee box, still wet with dew and barely enough light to see the flagstick, there were footprints.

As he began to start his round one morning, with the sun just starting to shine through the trees, he caught sight of a solitary figure on the first green.

"This must stop," he said to himself, and set his mind to catch the thief who stole his prized round of golf and confront this nemesis that had caused him so much anguish only by leaving footprints throughout the earth.

He teed up a ball and rushed through his tee shot. But no matter how efficiently Rodger played, he could never catch this shadowy golfer. At times he played so fast that his game could have been mistaken for a polo match played without horses.

Nearing the end and preparing for his approach at the 18th hole, Rodger saw the head groundskeeper standing just off the green, watching him. A perfectly struck 9-iron landed his ball a foot from the cup. *A birdie for sure*, he thought. As he approached the putting area, the greenskeeper tended the flagstick for him, then Rodger sank his putt.

"Well played, sir," the man said.

"Thank you. Um, do you happen to know who was playing in front of me today?" Rodger asked hesitantly.

"I do, sir. Why do you ask?"

"Well, to be honest, I've been trying to be the first person to play the course each day for the last several weeks. I was told the golf is better in the morning, and that it improves your health and decreases your score, and you complete a round faster."

"I know that to be true, sir."

"Ha," was all Rodger could say.

"You say you've been out here at the crack of dawn for several weeks?"

"Yes."

"In your round this morning, did you find yourself tired from the walk?"

"Not at all. I felt quite invigorated. In fact, I was running at times, and without losing my breath."

"Have you played better than usual?"

Grabbing the scorecard from his pocket he quickly marked the score for the final hole and tallied the round. "Yes," he said emphatically, "by three strokes today."

"It's barely morning. You must have played rather quickly today," the greenskeeper spoke, looking about the empty links.

"By Jove, I did complete my round faster than ever before."

"Well, sir, it seems that your early morning rounds have accomplished everything you've set out to do."

"I'll be. That's amazing. But, I have to ask. Who was playing right in front of me?"

"Well, sir, that would have been me. I always go out first. I play my golf as I tend to the tee boxes, set up the flagsticks, and brush off the benches for the members. I always knew what time you'd be starting as the club attendant informs me so I can make sure the course is ready for play before that time."

"Ha," Rodger laughed again.

"Sir, will you be continuing your early morning rounds or can I start to sleep in again?"

A Man's Game

ROSE HAD INSISTED her cousin, June, spend the summer at her golf club, stating that the fresh air and an occasional swim would be wonderful for her physical and mental health. After much coaxing, June agreed.

From the moment that young June arrived at Fox Forest Golf Club, she was the center of attention of all the men. Being a lovely and young woman, she was immediately asked to fill vacancies in any men's group for a round of golf. Having never swung a club, though, June had to respectfully decline.

After dispatching dozens of rejections, June was then offered golf lessons by every eligible male club member. Not one to decline an opportunity to try something new, and appreciating the attention, she accepted the offers and began her study of the game called golf.

Within a few short weeks June was playing several rounds a day, enjoying the outdoors and much doting from her male playing partners. After these rounds she would rejoin her cousin for dinner and they would chat about their day.

Soon thereafter, June was invited to dine with the men. Not wishing to insult anyone, she began accepting periodic invitations. Then, afraid of offending others, all requests were accepted. It was believed that June had every meal booked for the next several years, despite her schedule of only staying the summer.

Greatly missing time with her cousin, Rose also took up golf. Unlike June, Rose focused her attention on the women's group, the

Endearing Women's Golfing Group, where they would play a few holes, have tea after the round, and focus on things more refined.

Rose would hear the women gossip about how June spent more time with the men than a lady should. It had become such a subject of conversation that the president of the women's group decided June should play some golf with those of the feminine persuasion, hoping to remind June how a lady should act. The task to invite June to their group, and ultimately gain an acceptance of the request, fell on Rose.

"June, dear," Rose said, "the ladies are talking about you, and not in a positive manner. It's not good to make them angry. You must accept their invitation. Not doing so could cause you to be banned from the course, or even the club."

"Oh, sweet Rose," June said. "They aren't members nor are they on the board to make such decisions. Don't fear for me."

"You don't understand the way the world works, June. These women are married to many of the men that have that power. And women have a way of making men change their minds and do things they don't prefer to do."

With that, June accepted the invitation.

~

The next morning, June met the executive committee of the women's league for breakfast. After which, she and the president, the vice president and the chairwomen of the greens committee started their round.

June enjoyed golfing with these women. They presented a very relaxed atmosphere, were easy to relate to and talk with, they provided insights into womanly things, and didn't rush their game. In fact, June was considering canceling all her tee times with the men to enjoy more time with this lovely group. After finishing, June thanked the ladies for their time and then went directly home to prepare for dinner as she couldn't wait to tell Rose of her experience and the new direction for her future.

Once seated, June talked incessantly, telling Rose about the challenging shots each player made, the putts that were dropped, the discussions enjoyed, and all the fun she experienced.

"I can't wait for another round. I plan on asking for membership to the women's league tomorrow," June stated.

"June, dear. I'm afraid you won't be asked to return, nor will you be allowed to join the organization," Rose interrupted.

Quite surprised, June asked why on earth she should not be welcomed back.

"It was the way you played," Rose explained.

"Why do you say such things? I played quite well today."

"Yes, you did score quite well. In fact, I heard you suggested the president buy you lunch given the strokes you beat her by."

"I also was told," Rose continued, "that on the tee box you hit a second ball when your first went into the trees, and without taking a penalty stroke. They said you called it a 'mulligan.' And it was stated you played your turn out of order, took practice strokes in the sandy areas, left unrepaired holes in the short grass after your shot had been played, picked up your ball when it was close to the hole without hitting it in, and used profanity when your shots went errant. Could this all be true?"

With a shocked looked on her face, June responded, "Yes, I did all those things – though I don't see anything wrong with those actions. That's how all the men play."

The Angel on Twelve

ON NEW YEAR'S DAY, after spending a very exciting yet relaxing evening on the beach counting down the last few seconds of the year, I decided the first day should start with a round of golf. The resort in Florida we were staying at housed its own golf course, so the opportunity was easily taken.

My father was quickly up for the challenge while it took some coaxing to wake, and motivate, my son. But soon our clubs were loaded in the car and we headed off for the short drive to the clubhouse.

It's always a good idea to call for tee times in advance, but we were driven. We soon wished, though, that we had taken the time to call the pro shop as we pulled into an empty parking lot. A small handwritten sign on the door read, "Closed until noon – Happy New Year."

"Now what?" my son asked.

I was too determined to have my first hours of the new year spent golfing than to let a little thing such as the course not being open to stop me. "We play," I responded, then turned and proceeded to walk to the first hole teeing ground, followed promptly by my father and my son.

I need to remember to pay the green fees afterwards, I said to myself.

We saw not a single soul as we began our round, whether it be too early on such a notorious morning for sleeping in or the fact that the closed sign scared off the others.

What a wonderful time we were having that morning. The sky was blue with a slight breeze, we had no other golfers to wait for nor were we delaying any group behind us. It was just me and two of the most important male figures in my life, enjoying quality time together.

We played well yet nothing memorable happened on the front nine holes. We still saw no one else as we made the turn to the back half.

The twelfth hole was a one-hundred-twenty-eight yard par 3, playing to an elevated green across a grassy valley.

My son currently had the honors and played first. A duck hook sent his ball left, landing on the edge of the fairway some fifty yards from the green.

My father sliced his shot to the right, as he had been doing most of the day, ending on the side of the hill just below the putting area.

I hit an 8-iron high, straight and true, right at the flag stick. The ball landed on the front of the green, took a large bounce, and then was out of sight due to the green being higher than our current view.

We turned and picked up our bags and began to walk towards the green. As we started up the hill, my son headed to the left while I went with my dad to the right. In no time, my dad's ball was found and a short wedge put him onto the putting area. He was thirty feet from the cup but at least he had a chance at par. Looking across the fairway I watched my son as he hit his ball onto the green, too.

We converged again as we reached the green but it became immediately obvious there was something wrong as we only saw two balls sitting on the short grass.

"Your ball has to be nearby. Maybe it ran off the back," my father said as he walked to check out that portion of the green.

"I'll look on the left side," my son quickly offered and headed in that direction. "Remember, Dad, you only have five minutes in which to find your ball or the USGA declares it lost and that means you must walk back to the tee box, hit another ball, and take a penalty stroke," he said with too much enthusiasm. "If that happens, I'll take the lead. And I'd hate to see that happen."

I headed to the right to search.

"Only two more minutes," I heard my son yell as I continued looking for what I considered a well-hit shot.

Looking up, I noticed an elderly man, sitting on the bench that was at the adjacent thirteenth tee box, wearing a very big smile. "Can't find your ball?" he asked.

Obviously, I said to myself. "Correct, sir. Did you happen to see it come this way?"

"You know," he began, "I was playing earlier but my game was the worst I'd seen in years and had decided to quit and put an end to my misery and try another day when I happened across this bench. Sitting down, I realized what a lovely day the Lord had made. Then I noticed your group start to tee it up and thought 'I'll stay and watch, maybe they are having better luck than I.'"

"That's very nice," I said, knowing the clock was ticking and my son was watching even more intently than he did last night. "But, did you see my ball?"

"Certainly. It was a beautiful shot."

"Can you tell me where I can find it?"

"Definitely. I tracked it the entire time."

"And where can I find it?" I asked with some aggravation.

"Well, your ball landed on the green, took a bounce, rolled right up to the flagstick and sat on the edge of the hole. I said to myself, 'God must really hate that guy, to let him come that close to a hole-in-one and not let him get it.' Just then, a single puff of wind from exactly the right direction came along and tugged at the flagstick just enough to let your ball drop into the hole. Check the cup for your ball, son. I'm here to say that God gave you that hole-in-one."

Now, the idea to look in the cup is so foreign for me that it's always the last place I look. And I normally only do that with the thought that someone picked up my poorly hit shot and dropped it in there as a joke. But at this moment, after hearing this story, my heart jumped into my throat and I darted off to verify his version of the events with the enthusiasm of a child on Christmas morning.

Without pulling the flagstick from the cup, I thrust my hand into the hole and found a ball. I quickly pulled it out and rolled it around in my hand as I looked for my hand drawn green line that I use for identification. I yelled out to my son and father, "It's in the hole! It's in the hole!"

We celebrated with claps on the back as I finally scored my first ace.

We then proceeded to finish our round. And as we completed the eighteenth hole we saw the clock and knew the clubhouse would be open. We went in for lunch, drinks, to pay our green fees and, of course, brag about my shot on twelve.

Upon entering the clubhouse, my son and my father both started bragging to the crowd.

"My dad scored his first ace today!" my son shouted.

"My son finally hit a hole-in-one," my dad boasted.

"And just think," I said to them, "I wouldn't have found my ball in the allowed timeframe if it hadn't been for that gentleman on the bench."

To that comment, my family returned puzzled and perplexed looks.

"What guy? There wasn't a single person out on the course the entire time we played. What did he look like?" my son asked.

"Um, I don't recall. I remember someone sitting on the bench and telling me how my ball ended up in the cup. But I don't remember anything about him," I said.

I started to wonder if this person really existed, if it was my imagination, or if it were actually my golfing guardian angel. In any case, some kind of miracle happened to allow me to have that hole-in-one.

The Perfect Round

I SET MY TEE into the ground of the first tee box and placed a ball on it to start my round. It was a perfect day for golf. The sky was blue with a few wispy clouds, a gentle, warm breeze blew across the fairways, the birds were chirping, and my son was with me.

My first drive of the day was perfect. A gentle draw landed my ball in the center of the fairway and it rolled out to the one-hundred-fifty yard marker. My son's tee shot landed just behind mine. A 7-iron placed my ball on the back edge of the green. I had a long downhill lag putt that finished a foot from the cup for a gimmie, earning par.

All day long my drives were straight, my approaches landed on the green, my bunker shots were clean, and all putts rolled true.

I've played this course so many times that I know every location of all the bunkers, where to fade the ball, where to draw it, where to lay up, and where to go for it. I've memorized each tee placement, cart path, and putting green layout.

Throughout our round, my son and I enjoyed every stroke and every step along the grounds, while we walked, talked, and laughed, each second becoming a memory.

The course was in an ideal condition. We found no unrepaired ball marks on the green nor divots in the fairway. There were no other golfers in front of us to delay our play, no group behind us to worry about, and we made good time through the first nine holes.

I felt energized as we made the turn, completing the front and heading straight to the tenth tee.

As we finished the eighteenth hole and headed to the clubhouse we knew we had played a great game while enjoying each other's company, and that this was a very special day.

"Look at that," I said as we reviewed our scorecard while sitting on the veranda and sipping iced teas. "We tied, and played a perfect round, shooting par on every hole."

We sat there and quietly enjoyed the outdoors, knowing that times like this are what make life worth living.

"Mr. Todd. Mr. Todd. I hope I didn't disturb you. Are you ready for your final treatment?" the voice said as I was wheeled down the hallway. "This should be your last chemo session. I'm very optimistic on your progress. Just relax."

I set my tee into the ground of the first tee box and placed a ball on it to start my round. It was a perfect day for golf.

The Unknown Member

EVERYONE at the club knew Howard. He was always working his short game at the practice green, located behind the clubhouse. As you teed off on the first hole or were finishing up on the tenth or eighteenth, you could count on seeing him.

Howard was a very friendly person. He would always wish you good luck as you began your round, ask how your game went as you finished, and would chat about anything if you sat on the veranda with an iced tea in the afternoon.

Even on the day of the club tournament, Howard was practicing his putting and telling all those playing to enjoy their day.

"Where's Dick?" Nicholas asked. "Why is he always late?"

"Don't worry. He may be tardy but he always makes it," Joseph said.

"Todd group, if you don't have your fourth within the next five minutes you will be eliminated from the tournament," said the club director.

"Ugh. What are we going to do?" asked Richard.

"Hey, I have an idea. What about Howard?" Nicholas suggested. "He seems to have his short game down at least."

"Anything so we can play," Richard said.

"Fine by me," Joseph agreed. "Hey, Howard," he yelled across the practice area. "Would you be our fourth for the tournament?"

"Definitely," Howard stated as he grabbed his clubs and hurried over.

"Our fourth is here," Richard said. "We're substituting Howard for Dick."

"Fine," the director said. "Your group is up next."

From the first drive, Howard was amazing. His tee shots were long and straight, his approach shots always found the green, he could get out of the bunkers with ease, his putting was something unearthly, and he never lost a single ball. Additionally, Howard's efforts motivated the rest of the group to raise their game to a higher level of play.

The Todd group won the cup with ease, beating the next place team by no less than nine strokes. Afterwards, at the awards banquette, Howard and the rest of his group sat together and had a most enjoyable time. They dined and drank and laughed for hours.

Many other members came by to congratulate them. In true sportsmanship form, Howard was given most of the credit as he was proclaimed to have been the team's anchor. That led to other members inviting Howard to play on their team for other competitions and leagues.

Before too long, you never saw Howard practicing as he was always playing, moving from one group to another, attending all the award ceremonies and high class events.

As the end of the season approached, Howard was the only candidate for player of the year. This award was quite a notable achievement and the most sought after by all members of the Fox Hunters Golf Club, although no one put up a fuss about Howard receiving the accolade as his performance was exemplary.

At the conclusion of the meal, Howard was called to the stage to receive his award.

"As all can attest and support, this year's trophy belongs to Howard," the emcee stated. After Howard took the cup and shook hands with the president, he continued speaking. "And as is customary, Howard will tell us about his initiation into this fine establishment and his earliest memories of the club. Howard!"

As the applause died down, Howard began his speech.

"Thank you very much for this fine award. And I'm most grateful to all of the wonderful members who have allowed me to play on this exquisite course, dine on superior food, and enjoy their company. I remember my first day walking through the front gates of the club. I was awed by the immaculate conditions. From that moment, I was in love and returned daily. And for twenty years I enjoyed spending my time on the practice facility until one day I was asked to fill in for an absent member. And since that auspicious day, my dreams have come true. For you see, I am not a member. I simply live across the street from the course and was friends with the head greenskeeper before he died. Two decades ago he said I could use the practice area anytime I wanted and I took advantage of that heartfelt gift every day since. I would love to join this prestigious organization one day, when I have enough money. Until then, thank you again for this honor and I'll see you all tomorrow at the practice area."

His First Round

"IT'S TIME you learned to play golf," Alan said. "We've talked about this for years and, as your best friend, I'm making it happen. I'm on my way to your house now. All you have to do is get dressed. I have a set of clubs you can use and I'll let you borrow my extra shoes. The golf bag is already filled with tees and balls, so you will have everything you need. No excuses. I'll see you in an hour. Ok?"

"Sure," was all Robert could say as he hung up the phone.

An hour later, Robert and Alan, and their friends Brennan and Mark, were all piled in Alan's car, along with four sets of golf clubs, heading out of town.

"This is going to be great! Epic, even. I called my buddy at Willow Valley Golf Course and arranged tee times for the four of us. I even had the slots before and after us blocked out so we have a little more space to ourselves since this is your first round. Afterwards, we're going to enjoy a steak dinner on the clubhouse veranda overlooking the course, have a few drinks, and bask in the memories of your first round. I can't wait," Alan said as they continued on their drive.

"This is gorgeous," Robert said as they finally arrived at the course and drove down the willow-tree-lined winding road leading to the clubhouse.

"Wait until you see the fairways," Alan responded.

"Isn't this a rather expensive course?" Robert questioned.

"Yes, but don't worry. We all pitched in and are taking care of your greens fees. We want your first time to be special," Brennan responded as the car entered into a parking space.

"You guys grab the bags and I'll check us in," Alan said as he exited the car and walked to register the group.

"We're here," Alan stated as he entered the clubhouse.

"Hey Alan," Richard said, from behind the counter. "You're all set. The starter is expecting you. Have fun!"

"Thanks, pal. I'll talk to you when we finish and let you know how it went."

After checking in with the starter and heading to the first tee, each person grabbed his driver and started warming up.

"This is going to be great," Alan repeated.

"I'll lead off," Brennan said before landing a well-hit drive down the center of the fairway.

"Don't worry, Robert. We don't expect you to play that well, and we will all be with you throughout the day to help you with every shot," Mark said as he prepared for his drive, which he too landed in the fairway, some two-hundred-fifty yards out.

Hitting next, Alan striped his drive down the middle and at a distance equal to the others. "Ok, Robert. You're up," he said. "Nice and easy."

Robert set his tee, placed his ball upon it, took a few practice strokes, and swung. His swing at the ball looked like he was cutting wood, having a very steep angle of attack that produced a worm-burner of a drive and only traveled about fifty yards.

"Don't worry about that. We've all had similar drives," Brennan said. "Let's just keep moving closer to the pin."

Robert's second shot wasn't much better, nor was his next six before making it to the green on the opening par-four hole.

"We're all on the dance floor now. Let's see you roll it, Robert. Just like putt-putt at Hawaiian Rumble," Mark said.

Robert's putting wasn't much better than his drives. His body seemed stiff and his movements awkward. And after four more strokes he sank his putt.

"One down, seventeen more to go," Robert said with a slight smile.

"Not bad for your first time. I'm sure you'll settle into your game soon," Alan said, as he, Brennan, and Mark exchanged looks of concern before following Robert to the next hole.

Throughout their round, Robert didn't improve. In fact, it seemed as if his swing was getting worse, if that could be possible. His drives continued to go no more than fifty yards and reached no higher than five feet off the ground, his irons hit more grass than ball, and his putting was similar to that of a toddler just hitting the ball with a stick. Even in the bunkers, Robert would take a half dozen strokes before gaining freedom from the sandy snares.

To make the experience worse, all the extra strokes by Robert were taking their toll on the timeliness of the round. The small padding they had before teeing off was used before the third hole was completed. Throughout their day no less than six groups were allowed to play through them to the next hole before each was soon out of sight. One of these groups was nothing less than four octogenarians.

The constant waiting and short distances by Robert's shots threw off the rest of the group's focus, increasing their own mishit shots, and raising everyone's scores.

"Well, I did it. I've completed my first round of golf," Robert said as he tapped in his ball on the eighteenth hole for a score of thirteen.

"Yup," the rest of the group said hesitantly, all wearing expressions of exhaustion and frustration.

"I think someone mentioned a steak dinner," Robert said gleefully, as they all trudged towards the restaurant.

Once seated, an awkward and long silence covered the table.

The silence was finally broken as Robert asked, "Does it always take seven hours to play eighteen holes?"

"No," they all said through mumbled voices.

"But it's ok," Mark stated. "This was your first time. I'm sure you'll get better."

"Robert, I'm really sorry, pal. I didn't realize it would be this much effort for you. I've never seen anyone struggle with the game so much. Please forgive me," Alan said.

"That's ok. I had some fun and I appreciate all of you doing this for me," Robert responded.

"Is there anything we can do to help if you want to try golfing again? Some lessons, perhaps," Brennan offered.

"Well, maybe. I do have a question."

"What's that?" Mark responded.

"Do they make left-handed golf clubs?" Robert asked.

For Love and Golf

AFTER THE DEATH of his wife, Robert was overwhelmed with grief. For months he struggled with the loneliness he felt. This feeling only intensified as the winter set in and the scenery turned gray.

Eventually, after months of torment, spring came and Robert found some solace being outside. Something about grounding to the earth helped calm his soul.

While cleaning his garage, Robert ran across his golf clubs. He hadn't played in many years but thought the game might provide some mental distraction while offering the opportunity for a long and healthy walk. And it did. The hours of play he spent kept him focused on the present, rather than the past. Although, shortly after the round was finished, his mind slipped to memories of a love lost.

One day, while preparing to start a solitary round, another golfer asked if he wouldn't mind playing with another.

Immediately, Robert knew the answer was a resounding no. Turning to address the individual only assured him it was impossible, for she was a golfing vision of beauty – a short, athletically built woman, with long blond hair that fell from a Titleist baseball cap, dressed as if she just stepped out of an upscale golf-attire magazine. She was wearing a perfectly fitting pair of tan slacks, accentuated by bright pink golf cleats and a crisply pressed rosy cardigan sweater.

"Can't decide?" she said, walking closer and closer. "Are you afraid I'm going to beat you badly?"

Nearly nose to nose, Robert, shaken by so many different feelings, reached out and kissed her. To his astonishment, she kissed him back.

Once parted, they introduced themselves to each other, stated their handicaps and which set of tees they prefer to play from, and decided to press on together with match play being the format. Robert gave her the honors, of course.

During the round, Robert played better than he had in some time. The distraction was just enough to keep him from overthinking each shot, despite his desire to impress her.

Heather's game was equally as impressive, and they played even with each other, one taking a stroke advantage for a short time then periodically losing it.

On the 18th hole, they each drained twenty footers for birdies, ending the match all square.

"That was a most enjoyable round of golf," Robert stated.

"I agree," Heather said. "And, with no winner, what shall we do?"

"We could continue the match, say, tomorrow?"

"I look forward to it," Heather replied as she gave him a kiss on the cheek. "You make the tee times. I'll see you, same time and same place," she said and headed off the green.

That night, for the first time in months, Robert slept quite well. There was no feeling of loss, only hope for the future and his newfound golfing partner.

The next day, as he had hoped, the round with Heather was equally as pleasant. They each played well, and started to make small talk. Soon, they were enjoying dinner in the clubhouse at a small table for two.

As their time together increased, so did their fondness for each other. It hadn't been long before they purchased matching golf bags, and entered several couples' tournaments and won. They constantly exchanged gifts of new golf ball sleeves or bags of tees, just the right height and color, of course. New putters were unwrapped for their one-month anniversary of dating.

"Another wonderful round, Heather. Shall we grab a bite to eat?"

"Sounds perfect, Robert, but ..."

"What is it?"

"I was thinking. I would like to invite a third for our round this Saturday."

"What? Someone else? Did I do something wrong?"

"No, dear. I want to invite your son. I think it's time I met him. And what better way to introduce me to him than while doing what brought us together?"

"Splendid idea. I'll make the arrangements. Now, let's eat."

Saturday came, introductions were made, and a wonderful round was played.

"It was very nice to meet you, Nicholas," Heather said after putts were sunk on the 18th green, then hugged him goodbye.

"You, too," Nicholas said as he headed off the green. "Meet you in the car, Dad."

"That went marvelously. I'm so excited but wish you didn't have to leave," Heather stated"

"Me, too, dear, but these visits home from college offer me only a small amount of time with Nicholas, and I want to hear what he has to say about you. I'll see you tomorrow?"

"Definitely. Make sure you bring an extra sleeve of golf balls. I hear the conditions are going to be terrible."

At the car, clubs loaded, Robert and Nicholas drove away. Robert thought the ride was strangely quiet. *He must be tired*, he thought. *I'll let him rest until we're home.*

Once through the door, Robert pressed Nicholas. "So what did you think of Heather?"

"I think she's a bad name to golf! She didn't fix a single ball mark, nor did she replace or seed any divot she made, she hit out of turn, picked up her ball on the green without marking it, and didn't tend a single flagstick. I think she may have even taken a stroke that she didn't count."

Aghast, Robert blurted, "I've never noticed any of this behavior from her. Maybe she was nervous, meeting you for the first time. Yes, that must be it."

"Whatever you say, Dad. I'm heading to my room. Thanks for the golf today."

"Goodnight, son."

The next day, Robert and Heather met for their normal Sunday morning round. Robert tried his best to relax and enjoy the golf but his focus was on her every action. Luckily, all day long Heather hadn't made a single breach of etiquette nor broken any rules. *It must have been a fluke, she must have had the nerves*, he thought.

"All square, my love, 17 and 0. The fate of the match comes down to this putt," Robert said as he watched Heather mark her ball, pick it up and clean it, then pick up her marker and set the ball down a foot closer to the hole than it had been.

Shocked, he watched as Heather putt the ball into the hole.

"I win," Heather said impishly.

Robert sadly spoke, "I'm sorry, my dear, I claim the hole. You didn't replace your ball in its' original spot. I must call the infraction. That's a loss of hole penalty."

"You are going to charge me with that violation? Your marker? Your caddie? Your partner, on and off the course?"

"I must. The grand tradition of the game requires it. And I'm afraid we should never play together again."

"I agree," Heather said, through wells of tears. "I tried to make it work, but your slice is too unbearable to live with for the rest of my life."

"Goodbye, Heather," Robert spoke.

"Goodbye Robert. I concede the hole," Heather sobbed and walked off the green, grabbing her golf bag, and heading to the clubhouse.

Robert stood, motionless and alone, on the putting green and watched as Heather disappeared out of sight.

"Match," he said sullenly before grabbing his golf bag and heading to his car, all the while wondering if she would come back, at least for the Pro-Z golf balls he was carrying for her.

The Acer Family

ANDY WAS THE FATHER of three wonderful kids. As any parent will tell you, the time spent with your children grows shorter and shorter as they age, meet new friends, and spend more time at school and at extracurricular activities.

As a national salesman, Andy was away from home frequently. When he was away he always missed his children. In an attempt to spend the most quality time with them he could when not traveling, he decided the family should take up golf.

Andy knew that golf was a game his kids could play the rest of their lives; it can improve physical fitness and strategic planning and increase mental toughness, would allow three to six consecutive hours of time being together, and occasionally allow for destination vacations. To further hook the kids on golf he bought them trendy golf apparel, snazzy looking equipment, and would always treat them to sodas and snacks throughout and after the round.

Andy could golf with just one child for that personal time, or have two or all three together for a family event.

This activity continued for several years. As the kids grew they became better golfers. Eventually, they each played for either their high school team or on junior leagues throughout the county.

The day came when his oldest, Ryan, scored his first hole-in-one. Ryan became quite a braggart about his accomplishment, being the only one in the family to have carded a one on a hole. He even created his own private group, called "The Acer's Club," complete with a crest. This sparked a family competition on who would be next to score an ace and be admitted to this prestigious group.

Later that same year, Matt, his second oldest, flew one into the cup and earned the privilege to join his brother's club. And that's when the serious ribbing started. Every round of golf began with, "Maybe today will be your day to get an ace," and always ended with "Better luck next time." Every par three was prefaced with, "Here's another chance to join 'The Acer's Club'."

Ryan and Matt even purchased plaques that displayed the golf ball used to score the ace and housed the score card from that round, complete with the date and name engraved.

Similar jibing continued for several months and became nearly a daily event.

"Hey, Matt. There's some dust on your hole-in-one plaque in the hallway," Ryan would say.

"Thanks, Ryan," Matt would reply. "Your ace award looks spotless."

Andy and his daughter, Tricia, took the comments in stride. But, as fate would have it, Tricia eventually earned her first ace.

Now the sides were uneven and Andy heard comments from everyone. In addition to his three children, his wife started razzing him. Andy even heard comments from the parents of his kids' friends asking when he would card a hole-in-one.

His children ruthlessly picked on their dad for the fact that they had earned an ace in their first ten years of playing but their old man, in his forty years, still hadn't carded one.

Truth be told, Andy enjoyed this teasing. It was always done with love and, when an ace attempt turned into a double bogey, concern and support was provided. More than a couple times on the course, Andy actually would try not to earn an ace for fear of losing this special connection with his kids.

While away on business, Andy had the opportunity to play some golf with a prospective client. On the fourth hole, a long par three, Andy hit a beautiful shot that headed right for the flagstick. A mixed feeling of hope and fear came over him as he watched the ball hit the fairway in front of the green, take a couple bounces, and roll over the front of the fringe and out of sight.

Once to the green, the group looked for Andy's ball for a few minutes until one of his partners called out, "I found it."

"Where?" Andy asked.

"Check the hole," his friend said.

Upon doing so, Andy turned white.

"Congratulations," everyone said as they patted him on the back.

Luckily, Andy was able to keep this ace a secret from his family as these clients lived several hundred miles from his home.

After the trip, life continued as it always had. Andy spent quality time with his children who chided him at every opportunity and always provided encouragement for any attempt for an ace.

As time marched on, his children went on to college and started their own families. The group golf never stopped but the frequency greatly diminished to just a couple rounds a year.

One fall afternoon, Andy came home from one of these outings, tired and sore.

"How'd you play, dear?" his wife asked.

"Fine. The kids beat me again," he replied. "I'm going to my office for a couple minutes."

"Ok. I'll have dinner ready soon."

Once seated at his desk, his muscles weary, he leaned back for a moment. Eventually, he sat up, opened his top desk drawer, moved a pile of papers, and removed a cigar box. He opened the lid and stared at the contents, which were a half dozen golf balls. He picked each one up slowly and rolled it in his fingers to read the handwritten notes:

Andy's 1st ace 06/07/10; "1" par-3 150 yds 08/13/12; Ace 09/26/12; Hole-in-one 05/24/13; #1 11/11/13; and Ace 04/21/14.

Each ball marked his silent victory that all golfers dream of achieving. Slowly, Andy returned the balls to their home, closed the lid, slid the box to the furthest part of the drawer, and covered it with random papers.

To this day, Andy has never let his kids know of the success he had on the golf course. His children continue to tease him, and he loves that they do, as he loves them, and he wouldn't change a thing if he could.

A Golf Haiku*

Trees, grass, air, earth, sun.
Hitting a little white ball.
Enjoying the game.

*A traditional Japanese haiku is a very short form poetry, consisting of 17 sounds, in three phrases of 5, 7, and 5 sounds, respectively.

†as played on the GolfSmarter podcast

Dating and Golf

GREG LOVED GOLF! He subscribed to multiple golfing magazines, watched matches on television and streamed them at work on his computer. He always knew who won each competition, and recognized every player on the tour by sight and knew their statistics and history. He played regularly on multiple leagues and in friendly weekend rounds with anyone he would encounter. Greg was athletic, playing baseball and basketball for his high school alma mater. Despite this dedication and physical ability, he wasn't a very capable golfer, sporting a rather high handicap.

When not golfing, Greg had a normal life. He had a day job, normal errands, and a girlfriend. Regarding the later, Greg had been dating a wonderful women, Jennifer, for several months. They spent many hours together doing a large variety of activities, everything except golf.

Every Saturday morning Greg would leave the house very early and spend the day at the course. He would have breakfast at the clubhouse grill, warm up on the driving range and putting green, play eighteen holes, have drinks on the patio, and dinner in the club restaurant, all before returning home. This pattern continued for months, until, tired of being a golf widow and alone every Saturday, his girlfriend asked to accompany Greg on the course.

"That's a sweet idea, Jen. But the guys I golf with are majorly into the sport. They don't tolerate poor golfing in any manner and aren't shy about telling someone what they think. I feel you'd be very uncomfortable and wouldn't enjoy yourself."

"So teach me how to play," Jen responded.

Knowing this was a discussion that wasn't going to die quietly nor one he could win, Greg agreed. "Fine," he said. "We'll start next weekend. I'll skip dinner with my friends after the round and I'll take you to the driving range."

"Wonderful! I can't wait. This is going to be great for our relationship, just you wait and see. Can I come on Saturday and wait at the clubhouse while you play?"

"Ok," Greg sighed.

All week long, Jen waited anxiously for the opportunity to share something that meant so much to Greg, until finally the day came.

"The clubhouse is there," Greg said, pointing across the dashboard, to the other end of the parking lot as the morning sun slowly spread across the fairways. "There's a restaurant inside where you can get yourself something to drink while you wait for me."

"Don't worry about me. I'll get some tees and I brought a good book to read. Just have fun and I'll see you after you finish."

"Ok," Greg stated, as he exited the car, grabbed his clubs, and headed to the starters shack as Jen walked in the opposite direction.

Once in the clubhouse, Jen found a table in a quiet area and ordered her tea. She didn't sit idle long, though. Soon after Greg's group teed off, she headed to the driving range. At first, she just watched every golfer from a nearby area away from the action. She saw what worked and what didn't, and committed that to memory. Jen even took slow practiced swings with an invisible club, trying to get the physical feel of the task. When she felt like nothing more could be learned here, she went to the pro shop and purchased several issues of golfing magazines and read them cover to cover. Eventually, her free time came to an end as Greg entered the clubhouse.

"Are you ready?" he asked, exhaustedly.

"Yes," Jen said as she jumped up and followed him out to the range.

Greg had purchased a small bucket of balls for her. He began the lesson with explaining each club, its use and shot distance, before handing her a wedge.

"Let's start with the short iron. They are the most forgiving," he said.

Jen then took the club, set a ball on the ground, and took a gentle swing, trying to mirror what she had seen and read. She repeated this a couple times with Greg watching.

"Not bad," Greg said. "You launched those shots a bit high."

"But they were close to the flag I was aiming at," Jen replied.

"Pretty close. Let's try a longer club," Greg said, handing her a 7-iron.

Again, Jen took several strokes as Greg watched.

"Not bad for a beginner. Your shots didn't go real far. Let's try the big stick and see how you drive the ball."

Jen took the driver, teed the remaining balls, and swung, hitting them out into the open area.

"You didn't get a lot of height on those," he said.

"Maybe next time I'll do better," Jen said, sadly.

"Honey, I don't think golf is your game. Maybe there's something else you can do," Greg said as he gathered the clubs, packed them back in the golf bag, and headed to the car, Jen following with her head hung low.

Eventually, the relationship ended and Greg and Jen went their separate ways.

A few years later, Jen's friend Christine called her, stating she wanted to take up golf and invited Jen to accompany her. "We could make it a girl's time," she added.

Jen wanted nothing to do with the idea, remembering how bad she was in her last attempt, and declined the offer.

In the weeks to follow, Christine would share with Jen how much fun she was having on the course and of the new people she was meeting and how great it felt to have the exercise. This sparked Jen's desire, so much that she secretly scheduled her own golf lessons.

"Hi, Jen. I'm Howard, your PGA golf instructor, and I'll be helping you with your swing today. You ready to have some fun?" asked Howard.

"I guess," said Jen.

"Let's just start slow. Here's a dozen golf balls. Just take your time, hit a couple balls with each club, moving through the set.

When you're done we'll talk about your strengths and discuss some areas to work on. Sound good?"

"Sure," said Jen.

"So, what did you think?" Howard asked after Jen hit the last ball.

"Well, my tee shots weren't very high and they had a tendency to start left then go to the right some. My middle irons didn't get very high, either, nor did they go as long as my drives, and my wedge shots went too high and very short distances. I suck," she said.

"Jen," Howard responded forcefully. "That 'tendency to go right' is called a fade, and it's a very good thing to have. Your middle irons aren't supposed to go as far as your driver and you did keep those shots in the fairway, and your wedge shots are supposed to go high and for a short distance. You have the most fluid swing I've ever seen and made great contact with every ball. You are a natural!"

The Millionaire's Caddy

"SO, DO YOU GET OUT GOLFING much?" Richard asked.

"Not anymore, I'm much too old," said Bill through slow speech. "But when I was young, I used to caddy at one of the local country clubs."

"I bet you have some good stories," Richard inquired, fishing for a good tale.

"You bet. Here's one. The year was 1952, I was eleven years old. I was sitting in the caddy shack, waiting for another go around the yard when the caddy master called me up to carry for a guest player. You always felt excited when you got called for you knew that three hours later you were going to have some cash in your pocket. When I saw I was to be looping for none other than millionaire William Hopkins, the man the Cleveland airport was named after the year before, I was ecstatic. I could hardly wait to see the size of my tip.

"We started our round and from the first drive I was working hard. With all his money, you'd think he could have afforded golf lessons, but this man was a terrible golfer. I spent more time in the woods than the squirrels.

"I hustled much harder than usual as I really wanted to make a good impression. I ran to ever shot, fixed every divot, and was always near Mr. Hopkins for whatever he needed. I even fished two of his balls out of the water.

"I was cleaning his clubs as he putt out on the 18th hole, so that when he was finished everything would be top notch and buttoned up.

"He handed me his putter, thanked me for a job well done, and reached into his pocket. The anticipation built inside me. I could only imagine how much I was going to receive from somebody that was so rich.

"When it finally came time to settle up and receive my gratuity he gave me a shiny new quarter.

"'Thanks,' was all I could say."

"I don't know much about the tipping level in the fifties," Richard said. "Was that the going rate?"

"Oh, no. I usually earned two bucks per round. I was heartbroken and a tad bit miffed. But times were tough and I was young and grateful for the job so I kept my mouth shut. Taking the coin, I headed back to the caddy shack."

"Well, I guess that's why the rich are rich. They keep all their money."

Death and Holes~In~One

IT'S UNUSUAL these days to find someone you truly love and who reciprocates the feeling. Fewer still are those couples that stay married after decades or for their entire lives. Even rarer is when these two people share common interests, such as golf.

But this exactly describes Pete and Cindy, a couple who had been married for forty years and golfing partners just as long. They were fun to be around, were always friendly, had smiles on their faces and nice comments on their lips, and were proficient enough golfers to not slow your group but not so talented as to win every round.

After retiring they headed south, where golf isn't a 3-month-a-year season, to a nice golfing community. For years, they enjoyed the locale and played daily with anyone looking to fill a foursome.

One day, Cindy earned her first hole-in-one. Everyone was so happy for her, including Pete. The community threw a special party, she received cards of congratulations, and her name was engraved on a plaque that was displayed at the community clubhouse. But after a couple weeks, things settled down and life went back to normal.

During a male-only outing with his friends, Pete was asked if he was ever going to catch up with his wife and card his own ace.

For some reason, the way this was said really irritated Pete. It then became an obsession of Pete's to earn his own hole-in-one. This task consumed him and was the focus of his every round of golf. He ceased to enjoy the game, became rushed at the par fours and fives, pushing to get to the par threes for another chance at his goal. During this period of time he became less fun to play with, to the point that fewer invitations to join other groups were received.

Cindy realized what was happening and tried to calm Pete by stating facts on the odds of getting an ace and how it wasn't a reflection of his golfing ability nor his manhood. All attempts were in vain, though.

Pete's attitude continued, all the while the number of friends and playing partners continued to decrease.

During one round, Pete teed off on a par-three hole.

"That was fat," he yelled, then grabbed his golf bag and walked off the tee box.

"It wasn't that bad. I'd expect you should be on the green or close. A par, for sure," Cindy said as the others made expressions of disgust to one another.

"I doubt it but I'm unsure. The elevated green makes it impossible to know," Pete complained as everyone walked off the teeing area.

Reaching the putting green each person headed into different directions towards their lies. All golf balls were found except Pete's, so the hunt began around the area.

After a few minutes of looking, Cindy suggested Pete look in the cup.

"Why? It was a terrible shot," he responded angrily, but did check to appease her suggestion.

"It's here!" Pete exclaimed with elation and amazement, nearly falling to his knees.

Word spread quickly of Pete's ace. Just as had happened to Cindy several months prior, he was showered with accolades and well wishes and his name proudly displayed in the clubhouse. With this event, Pete's demeanor changed and life became friendly again and continued that way for many years until, sadly, Pete passed away.

There was no golf the day of his funeral as everyone in the community came to pay their respects. The greenskeeper even changed the golf flags to black, pulled them from the cups, and laid them on the putting green of each hole.

Cindy spent the day talking with everyone that gave condolences. She heard many stories about times each person spent with Pete. She knew these tales already as Cindy was generally at his side.

"I'm so sorry about your loss, dear," Sally said after giving her friend a warm hug. "He loved you and all the time you two spent together. At least he scored a hole-in-one before he died."

"I will truly miss him," Cindy said. "But I have a confession. I put his ball in the cup. Pete's shot didn't even make the green. I was desperate. His obsession was destroying our marriage, our life, our friends, and our golf. I moved his ball from the edge of the fringe into the hole while everyone was searching for their own shots."

The Loud Round

"ABSOLUTELY, we can get you on the course," the ranger said. "But we're pretty crowded so you'll need to play with another person. There's no more room for singles today."

"Sure, anything. This weather is perfect and I've been dying to hit the links," I said.

"Then I hope you're warmed up because your partner is getting ready to tee off any minute. Hurray to the first tee. You'll be playing with Mr. Filler. Oh, and by the way, we're doing a little construction around the course today. Sorry about any distractions. Enjoy your round."

"Thanks," I said as I exited the clubhouse and started jogging towards the opening hole.

Nearing the tee box, slightly out of breath, I waved a hand to get the attention of Mr. Filler.

"Hi, I'm Richard. The ranger said I'm to play with you this round."

Mr. Filler responded with a simple nod and went back to his pre-shot routine before letting loose his first drive of the day, which sailed down the left side of the fairway before drawing slightly and settling in the center of the fairway.

"Nice shot," I exclaimed to which I was met with another quiet nod.

Friendly guy, I thought as I set my ball and drove my own tee shot, landing just behind his.

We played quietly the rest of that first hole, exchanging no comments nor friendly words.

At the next tee box, I witnessed the work the ranger warned me about. A maintenance individual was cutting a fallen tree. The sound from the chainsaw was quite loud yet Mr. Filler appeared to not notice. I, on the other hand, was greatly disturbed and shanked my drive into the water that bordered the right side of the par three.

"Great," I mumbled and re-teed, landing my provisional ball on the front side of the putting surface. Again, we took turns and putt out in silence.

As I prepared for my approach shot on the next hole I was met with more distractions. No more than ten yards away the broken branches that lay on the ground under the tall maple trees were being picked up and mulched by a large and loud grinder. I tried to focus on my shot but I couldn't and topped the ball, sending my ball only twenty yards out into the fairway.

Annoyed with my poor performance, I watched Mr. Filler make a smooth and gentle stroke, hitting his ball perfectly and leaving it five feet from the cup. *This man has the focus of a laser*, I thought.

A few holes later, as I lined up a putt for par, the sound of a utility cart backing up was heard from a nearby area. That repetitive and high-pitched beeping sound is great to alert those nearby so they aren't run over but it wreaks havoc when trying to concentrate. I missed my putt and carded a bogey. Mr. Filler, though, seemed oblivious to the noise and drained a lengthy birdie putt. *He is rather impressive*, I said to myself.

And so it continued throughout the round. The ranger wasn't kidding. I've never seen so much maintenance activity on a golf course. And the noise was something that couldn't be easily overlooked, or overheard in this case. Yet, Mr. Filler had no trouble blocking these audial distractions from hurting his game – whether it be the leaf blower on the 5th hole, the stump grinder on 11, the mowers on 7, 13, and 15, nor the water pump on 17.

While putting out on the last hole we were once again met with distractions as the returned carts were being pressure washed and a mower was cutting the practice putting green.

As I had come to expect, I missed my putt and Mr. Filler played as if he was the only person on the course. I had to know how he kept such focus so, after our golf balls were holed, I questioned him.

"Tell me how you've managed to avoid all these terribly loud distractions today. I couldn't wrap my head around my game from all the noises, but you've done quite well," I asked with a look of hope and exasperation, staring at Mr. Filler.

"What did you say?" Mr. Filler replied. "Wait a second," he said as he reached into his pocket to produce two small objects, which he promptly pushed into his ears. "Sorry, I didn't have my hearing aids in. I can't hear anything without them."

Golf is Like Bowling

"On the way home from my daughter's 'Him and Her' Girl Scout bowling outing, I realized I'm just as bad a bowler as I am a golfer. Both my scores are around 100!"

Filling the Foursome

RICHARD AND CHRISTINE loved golfing together but, after many years of just twosomes, found themselves wanting to share their time on the course with others.

"So, do we want to take up another sport?" Richard asked.

"Of course not," Christine replied. "Let's see if we can find another couple we can golf with. How hard could that be?"

"What do you think about the Wadges?"

"No, Deanna has a bad hip."

"The Jenkins?"

"They're out of town every weeekend."

"How about the Todds?"

"Seriously?"

"I'm out of ideas. Do you want to take out an ad?" Richard jokingly suggested.

"Not a bad idea. There are a couple local golf courses with newsletters. I'll put in a listing and see where it gets us," Christine replied.

A week later, Richard and Christine had their first blind golf date with who, they hoped, would be their new best golfing friends.

"Nice to meet you, Jim," Richard said as he extended his hand.

"Good morning, Carol," Christine said as they embraced each other.

"Ready for some great golf?" Richard rhetorically said. "Go ahead, you can have the honors."

Jim teed his ball and hit the longest drive Richard had ever seen. Carol followed, also smacking one way out there.

Richard played next, landing his tee shot 50 yards short of Carol's and 100 yards short of Jim's drive.

"That all you got, Richard?" Jim said.

Once to the putting green, Carol taunted Christine. "I can't belive you missed that putt," she said as Christine left a two footer short. "My grandkids could sink that and they aren't walking yet."

"Maybe you two should hit from the kid's tees," Jim said as Richard prepared for his drive on the second hole.

This condescending banter continued throughout the round.

"I think we can cross them off the list," Richard said to Christine later that night, once they were alone.

"Definitely. What arrogant people," Christine replied. "I set up a round with another couple for tomorrow, just in case this were to happen."

The next day, Richard and Christine once again met their playing partners at the tee box.

"Nice to meet you, Kate," Christine said.

"Looks like we're going to have some great weather today, William. Why don't you and the Mrs. take the honors," Richard offered.

"The USGA states order of play is to be random. We're supposed to draw lots to see who goes first," William respond then stuffed four golf tees of differing length in his hand. "We'll play according to length of tees picked, with longest going last," he said while extending his hand towards Richard.

Richard drew the shortest one and teed his ball and swung. "Nice," he said aloud, remaking at one of his better drives. "I'll take it."

"Sorry, Richard. You put your ball into play from outside the tee box by an inch. You must replay the shot and assess yourself a two-stroke penalty."

"Right. Thanks for pointing that out," Richard said, as he teed another ball. Unfortunately, his second shot went half the distance of his first stroke.

"Christine," Kate stated a few holes later, "you must mark your ball before picking it up off the putting green to clean it. That's a one-stroke penalty to you."

Without fail, William and Kate continued their attention to legal play through the rest of the round.

"Well, that went even worse," Richard exclaimed once he and Christine were in their car.

"What rules freaks," she replied. "Wanna try again?"

"Sure. You never know."

Hoping for a different result, another round was scheduled the following day.

"Hi. Sorry we're late. Lunch took longer than expected. We got to talking and, well, that doesn't matter. I'm Joe, this is Sandy."

"Good afternoon. The ranger is pressing us to start, so do you want to play first?" Richard asked.

"No, no. Please, go ahead. It doesn't matter to us," Sandy retorted.

"Ok," Richard said as he led off the group, with Christine promptly following.

"You're up," Christine said.

"Sorry, I'm still getting ready," Joe said as he sat and tied his shoes.

"Sandy, are you ready to play?" Richard asked.

"Just another minute. I need to warm up a bit more," Sandy responded as she twisted back and forth before starting deep knee bends. She continued her calisthenics for another couple minutes before putting her ball into play.

At the next tee box, Richard, Christine, and Sandy all hit onto the green of the short par-three second hole. Suddenly, they were startled by not seeing Joe ready to tee off. Looking around they found him sitting on a nearby bench.

"Nice day," he said. "I thought I'd just take it in. Oh, is it my turn? Just give me a minute to go get my club and wash my golf ball."

A few holes later, as the last putt was in the hole, scores started to be exchanged and documented.

"Where's Joe?" Richard said, looking around.

"There," Christine responded, pointing to a small pond by the side of the putting green.

"Hey, I thought I'd pick up a few extra golf balls while we're here. There's tons of 'em just lying around," Joe said, pointing to the bank with his ball retriever.

Many hours later, they parted company and left the final hole.

"That was grueling," Christine said. "Their pace of play was terrible."

"Absolutely," Richard responded. "Anyone else on the list?"

"Yes. Tomorrow afternoon."

"Ok. At least we can have a nice meal before we play."

~

"Good afternoon. I'm Richard and this is Christine."

"Hi, Gary and Linda. Nice to meet you two."

"Let's golf," Richard stated. "I'll play first," he said then teed his ball.

"Nice round, Gary. And tight match," Richard stated eighteen holes later. "If I hadn't had that birdie on the tenth hole, you and Linda would have beat us. What do you say, a rematch next week?"

"To be honest," Gary hesitantly spoke, "we find you two to be a tad arrogant, a little rules obsessed, and your pace of play doesn't match ours. I think we'll pass on the offer."

"Oh, ok. Um, goodbye, then."

Richard and Christine watched Linda and Gary walk towards the clubhouse as they stood, dazed, on the green. Richard regained his senses first and turned to Christine.

"What do you think, dear? Golf, tomorrow, tee time for two," Richard said, slyly.

"Absolutely," Christine said with a large smile. "Only you and me, eighteen holes, and just the way we like it."

The Club Dinner

"I CAN'T BELIEVE we received invitations to the club for dinner," Steve stated.

"I'm amazed, too. It's not like we're the newest members," Andrew responded.

"And we're definitely not the best golfers. I'm sure our handicaps are some of the highest," Richard added.

"So why did we get invited and why is the dinner being held in the winter?" Steve asked.

"Beats me, but I can't wait to get there. Its nerve-wracking driving in this snowstorm. I can barely see the road," Richard said. "This drive is long in the summer, so it's going to take us hours to get there in this weather."

"At least in the summer it's sunny when we're heading to the course to play golf," Steve said. "I never noticed there are no street lights on the drive."

"Whose idea was it to build a course in the middle of nowhere?" Andrew asked.

"Read me the invitation again, Steve," Richard said. "It will help pass the time."

"Sure," Steve replied as he opened the calligraphy-addressed envelope. "You are cordially invited to Crystal Mountain Golf Club for a special event. Dinner will be prepared by the club's new chef and will be served at 7:00PM. Cigars and brandy will be served immediately afterwards, fireside, in the library. RSVP not required."

"Sounds great," Andrew responded.

"Definitely," Richard said. "And, look, we're at the gates. And they're open! I wasn't looking forward to getting out of the car to swipe my key with the way the snow is blowing."

"Check it out. The road is clear. The grounds crew is really on their game. They must have just finished plowing. I'd love to see them driving a big truck down this winding lane. I wonder how many trees they clipped. There's not much room on either side," Andrew said.

"Finally, we're here," Richard exclaimed as he parked the car then let out a big sigh.

"I don't see anyone else in the parking lot. Looks like we're first to arrive. Doesn't surprise me with this snow. I wonder if they're going to delay eating," Steve said.

"Let's just get inside," Andrew said as he exited the car quickly, ran to the large oak doors, and entered the foyer.

"Hello," Richard called out after seeing no one.

After a lengthy silence Steve spoke. "Well, we're here for dinner. Let's head to the dining room."

"Maybe it's cancelled. There's no one in the dining area and the tables are all covered," Andrew stated, looking down the hall.

"There's a light on in the private meeting room," Richard said as he headed in that direction. "Follow me."

Upon entering the private area, reserved for board members, special guests and VIPs, and special events, it was observed the table was set for dinner with an elegant display of fine china plates, covered with metal warming domes, and accented by exquisite cutlery and glassware.

"Wow! I've never even seen this room let alone eaten in here," Steve said as he sat at the table.

"Should we wait?" Andrew hesitantly asked aloud.

"The table is set with just three plates and we don't want our food to get cold. I think we should start. With this weather, you never know when or if anyone else will arrive," Richard said then uncovered his plate to reveal an exquisite presentation of a perfectly prepared filet mignon gently garnished with tender young asparagus, accompanied by a twice-baked potato, and paired with a petite lobster tail.

"Looks great! Let's dig in," Steve said as he grabbed his fork.

At the end of the meal, everyone sat back in their chairs, extremely content, resting and enjoying the flavors that still muddled in their mouths.

"That was one of the finest meals I've ever had," Andrew stated.

"Has the fireplace been lit the entire time?" Steve asked as he noticed the flickering flames from the hearth that was in the adjacent library.

"I don't remember. I was too focused on the food. Let's check it out," Andrew said as he stood and moved from the table, followed by Richard and Steve.

"Very nice," Steve said as he sat in one of the three leather winged-back chairs facing the fireplace.

Andrew also sat then noticed a bottle of Benedictine, three crystal rock tumblers, and a cigar humidor on a small stand between the chairs.

Leaning forward, Richard looked through the French doors leading back to the dining room. "Hey, the table has been cleared. I didn't hear or see anyone take care of it," he said.

"Like I said before, the staff is on their game tonight. Relax," Andrew said, handing him a cigar.

Richard complied. Leaning back in his chair he let out a long exhale of smoke.

"That's one of the best stogies I've ever had," Steve added.

With the meal finished, having settled into extremely comfortable chairs, each person relaxed and enjoyed the fine cigars and vintage liqueur.

After some time, Richard straightened up in his chair and stared inquisitively at his companions. "How long have we been here?" he asked.

"I'm not sure. Seems like hours," Steve replied.

"And during all that time have we seen anyone else?"

"No."

"No one. We've not seen, or heard, anyone plow the roads, serve the food, light the fire, clear the dishes, or set out the decanter and cigars."

"So. What are you getting at?" Steve replied.

"Remember the terrible storm we drove through?" Richard questioned.

"Of course," Andrew replied.

"What if we didn't arrive here safely? What if we actually died in a car crash on the way to the club and this is heaven, or purgatory, or something?"

Steve and Andrew looked at each other with perplexed expressions for a moment.

"I think you've had too much to drink," Steve said as he took another sip from his glass.

"I'll be right back," said Richard, then left the room and wandered around the clubhouse for several minutes.

"There's nobody here," Richard said as he returned.

"I'm sure the staff headed home. Remember how bad the snow was coming down," Andrew stated.

Richard then headed to the window, pulled back the curtains, and looked out. "Wow. The snow is at least a foot deep," he said.

"Then we're not going anywhere," Steve replied. "Sit down. Have another drink."

Richard topped off his glass and made himself comfortable again in his chair, resigning his comments as folly.

The hours crept by as the three enjoyed the evening.

"That's it, I'm spent. I'm going to sleep," Richard said as he got up and staggered towards the hall.

"Where are you going?" Steve mumbled.

"There are some couches in the lounge. I'm going to sprawl out until morning."

"Ok," Steve said, finally pulling himself to his feet. "Hey, Andrew," he said, smacking his feet and waking him from his nap. "Come on. We're moving to the couches."

Finding areas to lie down, each person promptly fell deeply into sleep.

The next morning, Richard was violently awoken.

"What is going on here?" a voice bellowed.

Sitting up abruptly, Richard saw the club president, Dick, standing in the door frame.

"I can't believe what I'm seeing! There are pots and pans all throughout the kitchen, dirty dishes on my dining table, cigar stubs and ash in the smoking trays, empty glasses everywhere, and is that my private store of Benedictine," Dick stated, pointing at an empty decanter lying on the floor next to Richard.

"No, it can't be," Richard muttered. "Everything was cleared by the staff."

"Staff, what staff?" Dick responded. "No one has been here all week. Get up! Get out of here, and don't come back – ever! I'm going to see that your membership is revoked. Now get out!" he yelled as he stormed out of clubhouse.

Puzzled, Richard fell back onto the couch and slipped into unconsciousness.

Sometime later, Richard, regaining awareness, could tell by the way the light entered the windows that it was late in the afternoon. Memories started to float into his mind like clouds across a sky.

"Was the club president here?" he asked aloud, unsure if Andrew or Steve was awake to hear him.

"No one's been here. Be quiet, my head hurts," Andrew replied slowly.

"Are you sure?" Richard asked. "You didn't hear him yell and expel us from the club?"

"We would have heard that. I'm sure we wouldn't still be lying here if that were the case," Steve replied.

Upon hearing these comment, Richard again laid down. Looking out as his mind drifted he saw several wet footprints on the foyer tile.

An Accidental Golf Career

"DAD, I WANT TO PLAY GOLF," Mike said.

"Really?" Frank questioned. "You've never been interested in that game before."

"I know, but Nicholas was telling me about the fun he has playing and I'd like to give it a try. Can you drive me out to the course so I can practice?" Mike asked.

"I'll do you one better. Why don't you take some lessons, so you will know what you're doing? And I'll accompany you. I've never played before, and this way we both can learn and maybe we can golf together a few times. You're more likely to get me to pay for your golf if I'm there, too," Frank said.

"Ok. When can we start?"

"I'm not scheduled to be on the air tomorrow so let me make some calls. We can buy some equipment and go from there. Sound good?"

"Sounds great!"

The next day, Frank and Mike purchased some discount clubs, bags, and balls, and took their first golf lessons, followed by a fun, yet very high scoring, round.

~

"Hey, Frank."

"What's up, Roger?" Frank replied.

"There's this local guy who wrote a humorous golf book about the rules. We'd like to put him on the air. You're the only one at the station that plays the game. Why don't you interview him?"

"Sure. I'll give it a shot, boss."

"Great. Thanks, Frank. His name is Richard. Have fun."

~

"After twenty years of talking to hundreds of thousands of people daily, I'm at a loss for words," Roger spoke. "We've made this radio station into something to be proud of but the new owners have a different vision for the future. I wish each of you the best of luck in whatever you do and I thank you for your years of service."

Outside the building, deep in thought while carrying a box of mementos from what was his office, Frank was brought back to reality as he heard his name.

"So, Frank, what are you going to do now that's we're all unemployed?" Mark asked.

"Well, I'm thinking about starting my own business. I've been considering some kind of marketing."

"Good for you. You should try, what are they calling it, podcasting. It's like radio, about which you are very knowledgeable, but with the internet instead of frequency."

~

Frank took that advice, and over the next thirty years interviewed thousands of individuals and groups in the golfing world. He talked with celebrities, dined with superstar athletes, golfed at the finest resorts and in tropical settings, and made a global name for himself, all the while recording his activities to share with the world.

One day, at a ripe age of ninety, Frank died quietly, surrounded by family in his home. His property bordered his favorite golf course, and was so close to the links you could hear golf balls land in the fairway. On this day, though, there was no sound – no laughter, no golf balls being hit, no clubs rattling in their bags, only the sound of the flags, marking the hole locations on each putting green, flapping in the wind,.

Frank was cremated and a small private funeral was held. Unbeknownst to the local course, his ashes were spread over the eighteenth green.

In the following days, his family continued on with life, although a tad slower and more quietly, until the postal carrier came to the door.

"I'm so sorry for your loss, Mrs. Green," he said.

"Thank you," she replied.

"Here's your mail. There's too many letters to fit in the mailbox so I brought them to the house."

"Really? Who are they from?"

"Lots of people. There are return addresses from many different states. There are even a few letters from outside the U.S.," he said, handing Joanne the armful of letters and walking away.

One by one, Joanne read the heartfelt correspondences, each one giving praise to Frank for the joy, guidance, motivation, and education he provided through his show. Some writers gave him credit for helping decrease their golfing handicap, others just for providing entertaining and lively content. One gentleman, a former amateur golfer now confined to a wheelchair, wrote how he so miserably missed the game but was comforted, for at least an hour a week, when he listened to Frank's show.

The obituary in the newspaper was lengthy, listing countless professional, civic, and humanitarian awards Frank had earned, the many selfless acts he performed that helped golf organizations worldwide, and many famous individuals he worked with that later became friends. And at the end of the article was a quote from the family:

> "Growing up, my dad always told us to find our passion and make it our life's work. He said if you did then you would always be happy. This describes what he did. Frank was joyful spending his days talking about golf to anyone who would listen, helping out anyone he could through a sport he loved, and sharing that fondness with family and friends. Golf offered him an opportunity to help others and provide for his family, and do so in a gratifying way. That is a lasting legacy we can all be proud of."

~

Golf gives everyone the chance to share a love of the game with the world and to be good citizens while doing so.

A Lawyer's Round

ROBERT AND MATT were two local, well-known attorneys. They were notorious because of their legal expertise and the high-profile cases they handled. Because of these combinations, they were both quite wealthy. So much, in fact, that lately they were seldom in the office, choosing to regularly play golf at the country club where they each belonged.

Matt and Robert played golf similar to the way they lived life, giving it their all and pushing the boundaries. They further enhanced their rounds with obscure challenges and large wagers against each other. They generally played only as a twosome as the rest of the members of the club stayed away from them, unable to keep up with their abilities or betting limits.

These lawyers were absolute in following the rules. Each was a stickler for every USGA Rules of Golf point. If there was any disagreement on the interpretation, a long and heated discussion surely would follow. A call to the USGA's rules committee was frequently placed to settle a dispute.

One day, Robert suggested a one thousand dollar competition, using the rules of match play.

Matt was never one to back down from a bet, nor was he one to be content with the challenge as provided.

"Fine," he said, "but we play everything down. Everything. Do you agree to the terms set forth?"

"I accept your counteroffer," Robert said, agreeing to the challenge.

Being nearly exact equals, the round was very competitive and the scores tight, with one player taking no more than a half-point advantage over the other before the match would square. This back-and-forth scoring went on for seventeen holes.

"Ready, Matt," Robert inquired, "to finish this round? I'm looking forward to spending your money."

"Definitely," Matt replied. "But I'm the one that is going to win. And it's my honor," he said as he teed a ball for his drive on the meandering par-four eighteenth hole. A powerful swing sent his ball towards the left side of the fairway, coming to rest near the cart path at the end of the hill.

"That's my longest drive of the day. Top that," he said.

Without a word, Robert set his own ball and began his pre-shot routine, eventually sending his drive on a mirroring path. The ball sailed down the fairway, coming to rest a few yards from Matt's ball but on the cart path.

"Looks bad," Matt said as he and Robert entered the golf cart and drove towards their lies.

Stopping a few yards before reaching their balls, Robert exited the cart and walked towards his lie and began to pick the ball up.

"What are you doing?" Matt asked.

"I'm going to move my ball off the cart path. The USGA allows me free relief," Robert replied. "Or have you forgotten the rules?"

"It's you who has a memory problem, my friend. Don't you recall our agreement to play everything as it lies?"

"You've got to be kidding me. You're going to make me hit my ball off the cart path?"

"Absolutely. Unless you want to announce me the winner of the bet, in which case I'll allow you to throw your ball into the fairway."

"Fine, have it your way. Can I take a practice stroke, though?" Robert asked.

"Sure," giggled Matt.

Robert then walked behind the golf cart, pulled out a 7-iron, returned to his ball, and took a practice stroke. His club made a loud grinding sound as it made contact with the pavement.

"Do you mind if I take another practice swing?"

"Take as many as you want," Matt said through chuckles.

Robert then took several more practice swings, each time skipping the bottom of his metal club off the pavement and causing sparks to fly.

"Ouch," Matt grimaced as Robert continued his practice swings before finally hitting the ball. The flight was perfect and the ball landed on the front of the green and rolled right up to the flag, took a pause then fell into the cup.

"I'll take the win for this hole and that's match for me. One thousand dollars, if you please."

"I can't argue with that shot. Before we settle, what club did you use?" Matt asked.

"Your 7-iron," Robert responded with a sneer.

"What? My club?" Matt said. "Those are custom fit and ground clubs."

"Really ground now."

"You owe me $500 for the damage."

"Fine. For the record, I owe you $500 for damage to your golf club," Robert responded. "And you owe me $1,000 for the match."

"Try again," Matt said. "You owe me $1,500."

"How do you figure?" Robert asked.

"By using my club, you added it to your bag, and now your club count is fifteen. USGA rule #4-4 specifically states there is a fourteen-club maximum. You have exceeded that limit and thus incur a penalty."

"Agreed. Standard two-stroke penalty, right? Go ahead. You have two strokes to hole out and that's not going to happen."

"Objection. Match play says your penalty is loss of hole. So the hole goes to me, and subsequently, the match. You owe me $500 for my club, and $1,000 for the match."

"Ugh," Robert resounded.

"You want me to buy you lunch?" Matt asked. "I just came into some money."

Golf Guilt

"WELCOME TO THE SHOW, Richard!"

"Thanks, Fred. It's great to be here."

"I have to say, I love what you've come up with. So many golfers are in need of this information and you've found a great way to present it in a funny, yet helpful, way. Why don't you tell our listeners about it?"

"I'd love to! So, my story starts thirty years ago. It was the first time my dad invited me to golf with him and his friends. I was feeling pretty proud that day. I managed to work through the first tee jitters, kept my drive in the fairway, and advanced to the green. At this point, I'm thinking *I can do this* and am ready to settle in for a fun day of golfing. To pull my weight with the group and impress my old man, I was tending the flagstick for him. He was just off the green with an awkward downhill lie. He skulled it and the ball was making a fast line for the hole. As I started pulling out the flagstick he begins yelling for me to put it back in. He's hoping the ball hits the stick to stop its momentum, using the pin as a backboard. Well, that didn't happen the way he wanted it. I didn't get the flag back in the cup, the ball ran over the hole, across the green, and down the hill. At this point, he begins yelling at me, blaming me for his new lie. And this wasn't done quietly. The rest of group and everyone on the nearby holes heard his rantings. I'm now feeling about an inch tall.

"Flash forward thirty years, my son wants to make the high school golf team. So when the sun is shining, he and I are out playing, working on his swing. At night, I'm reading the rule book so I can give him some coaching.

"One night, I was reviewing the section on tending the flag stick and realized that, all those years ago, I acted properly in the way I tended the flag. My father was wrong and had no grounds to chastise me.

"It made me furious that I carried that golf guilt for three decades when it wasn't necessary. I thought there has to be a better way for golfers to learn the rules than as secondhand information from someone else when that person generally doesn't know the rules in the first place. As golfers, most of our education comes from family and friends. In what other situation would we ever take advice from most of these people?

"I realized that this example clearly explains the proper way to handle this situation. As I read more of the rulebook I recalled more examples that mirrored the procedures. I then had the idea to string together all of these examples into one story of an entire round to educate while entertaining. The result was *The Golf Rules*, which I then turned into a series that covers stroke play, match play, and golf etiquette."

"Amazing, Richard. What then?"

"With this vision, I started my writing career. I went to workshops, took online writing courses, contacted the USGA about rules reviews, attended a PGA/USGA school, and began looking at publishing options. Three years later *The Golf Rules* was sitting on the shelves at the bookstores."

"What a wonderful ending."

"It's no ending. though, it's just the beginning. Through speaking engagements, author events, and book signings I've met a lot of great people and heard many wonderful stories that led me to write another series called *Short Stories from the Long Links*, which is a collection of golf-related tales. It's been a lot of fun! I have readers from many different countries and have been contacted by loads of people that learned the proper way to handle the rules and act on the course and who have enjoyed the stories I've published."

"That's great. I'd love to hear more but we're out of time. Before you leave, please tell everyone where they can find your books and how to get in touch with you."

"You can find all my products at Amazon, Barnes & Noble, select golf stores, and on my website, www.TheGolfRules.com. You can also see information on me, my books, and my events there. I can be followed on Facebook, WordPress, YouTube, and Twitter. Email me at Richard@TheGolfRules.com. Thanks for having me on," Richard concluded.

The Perfect Date

I'VE BEEN GOLFING for over forty years and married for more than half of them. And each time I've headed out for a round of golf, I felt a little awkward leaving my wife by herself at home for a full day. She'd never said anything but her body language and tone stated something different.

One evening, over dinner, she says to me, "Doug, I want to go golfing with you." Since she had never shown interest before, and seeing a way to alleviate some guilt, I welcomed the idea. We discussed dates and agreed on an early Wednesday morning round, before the course was crowded. Just the two of us and eighteen holes.

Lorie already had brand new equipment as I had given her a full set of clubs and a pink cart bag several years ago, for her fortieth birthday, so there wasn't much to do except make tee times. In preparation for our "date," she pulled the bag from the closet and removed and inspected each club from the bag, which were still wrapped since the day she received them.

We started out that auspicious morning with an early breakfast at the clubhouse grill. I like to begin a day of golf like this; it fills your belly and puts you in the golfing mindset. After our meal, we stepped outside to prepare for our round. It was a gorgeous fall day with a bright blue sky and a gentle and warm breeze blowing. There were few other golfers about.

"Apparently everyone is home doing gardening," my wife stated.

The grounds crew had done a great job of keeping all the brightly colored leaves off the fairways and greens. What was left on the trees provided a colorful backdrop for our round of golf.

My wife played well enough, considering she hadn't played in decades, and having her nearby kept me from getting angry at my missed and poorly hit shots that would have normally ruined my round.

She complimented me when I had hit the mark and was supportive when my ball went to the bottom of the ponds, and I did the same for her. We didn't keep score; instead we just enjoyed a leisurely walk in a predefined pattern while hitting a little white ball from one area to another.

Once finished, we again visited the clubhouse and enjoyed a tall cool beverage and a tasteful lunch while sitting on the patio that overlooked the back nine, appreciating the scenery of the grounds we had just walked, while listening to the football game that was being broadcasted through the outdoor speakers.

As we drove away from the course, I couldn't help but think how perfect this day was. I spent time with my best friend, engaged in some physical activity, challenged my body and mind, enjoyed the perfect outdoor conditions and views, partook of some very enjoyable food, and listened to some sports. I wondered how often Lorie wanted to have these perfect dates and if my Saturday rounds would be shared with her instead of my normal playing partners.

Once home she began to tell me how delightful the day was for her.

"I enjoyed it too," I responded. "When do you want to go out again?"

"Well, I think I'm done with golf," she replied to my amazement.

"Really? Did I do something wrong?" I questioned.

"Not at all, dear. The day was perfect. I can fully appreciate and understand why you so enjoy the sport and spend so much time playing. It's a perfect combination of exercise, competition, camaraderie, and the outdoors. Golf just isn't my game. I'm not a big fan of the heat and I found it a bit frustrating. Maybe we can go out in another twenty years."

"Sure thing," I responded supportively.

~

She never did golf with me again, but we did have that one memorable round that I will never forget. Golf is like that.

The following Saturday I restarted playing with my regular group and enjoyed every round, most of the time. Although my fondest memory was that one spent golfing with the love of my life.

A Temporary Love Affair

PHILLIP WENT THE FIRST THIRTY YEARS of his life without every touching a golf club. He never had the opportunity as a child, nor the time while in college, nor the desire as a newly married man.

Soon after starting a new job, his employer asked him to move to Texas. Being young and ready for adventure, he and his wife packed up their meager belongings and left Ohio.

As they settled into their new home, they began to become involved in the community, learn the area, and meet new friends.

One of Phillip's friends, Richard, was an avid golfer and pressed Phillip nearly daily to come on a round with him, touting the benefits of a good walk, the social aspect, and the competition against yourself and others.

Before Philip could accept one of the many invitations, he and his wife once again moved so that Phillip could accept a new position, one at the corporate office. They packed, said goodbye to their friends, and left to return to Ohio.

As life continued Phillip was asked by his new neighbors to join their golf league, promising an enjoyable round. Phillip, not motivated to start a new sport, declined the invitations, giving a variety of excuses, including the lack of equipment.

"Just a minute, Phillip, I'll be right back," Mark said, then walked to his house next door and returned with a golf bag full of clubs. "I have an extra set you can have. They were given to me and now I'm giving them to you. How about this Saturday afternoon we try them out?"

"Fine," Phillip stated under duress. "I'm not going to be any good. Just so you know."

"We'll fix that, don't worry. See ya later," Mark said as he headed back home.

That weekend Phillip played his first round of golf and, as expected, he performed extremely poorly. But, with the support and encouragement from Mark, he continued. Phillip spent time at the driving range, took lessons, read up on the rules and etiquette of golf, and slowly improved his game and grew in his love for the sport.

He and Mark played regularly for a few years until Mark moved out of the state.

Phillip continued playing, going out by himself the rest of that summer. And as anyone from the northern states knows, there is a long span between golf seasons while lots of snow sits on the ground.

The next year, spring came but Phillip lost his desire to play. The clubs that were gifted to him sat in the garage, unused, for a couple seasons.

As the garage and home filled with items no longer used, Phillip and his wife hosted a garage sale to clear out the clutter.

During the sale, a young boy inquired about the golf clubs sitting in the corner, not marked for sale. Having no use for them, Phillip decided to pass them on.

"Tell ya what, you can have them for free. Just make sure you use them, enjoy the game, and give them to someone else when you are done with them. Ok?"

"Deal. Thanks mister," the youth said, enthusiastically.

Years after that garage sale, Philip, still having not returned to the game, wondered how the clubs were doing and fondly remembered how those sticks would perfectly hit shots that rattled flagsticks while he meandered through wooded acres.

The Salesman's Handicap

GROWING UP I HATED GOLF. My old man was a salesman, and back in the '50s that meant a lot of traveling by car. My dad was a single parent and, with me only being ten years old, that meant I spent many hours in the backseat. Remember, this was long before Wi-Fi, the internet, and anything electronic that could help keep my interest. We didn't have a lot of money so my dad would allow me to roam about, "near the car" as he would say, when he was busy with clients.

So why did I dislike golf? Most of my father's "meetings" were held on golf courses. It was an age when that type of business was acceptable and routine.

While he played I was able to walk about the practice area or watch other golfers start their rounds on the first tee box or finish up on the last hole. Usually I stayed in the parking lot, close to our car. All this was quite boring, supporting my dislike for the game.

As the old saying goes, a person's handicap was equal to the number of hours they spent in the office. So if you were very proficient at golf, having a low handicap, you were assumed to spend few hours at your desk actually working, and vice versa.

Well, my old man must have hardly ever been outside the workplace as I never saw him win a match. Ever.

After every meeting, and by that I mean golf game, he would get back in the car and I would ask him if he won. The answer was always, "Not this time, pal." He really should have said, "Not ever, I suck." This was just another reason why I showed little interest in the game during my youth. And so this cycle continued for years until I was old enough to stay at home by myself.

One day, while home alone and rummaging through the garage, I came across a few old golf clubs of my dad's.

"How hard can this game be?" I thought to myself and picked up the wedges and a couple balls and headed to the back yard. From that first pitch shot, which landed in the sandbox as desired, I was completely and emphatically in love with the game. I practiced often and played with friends. I didn't speak of this to my dad. Knowing how poorly he played. I didn't want to make him feel bad.

One day, he came home early from a trip and spotted me in the yard practicing some flop shots.

"Hey, I didn't know you liked golf. Since I'm home sooner than expected and there's plenty of daylight, what do you say you and I go out and play a quick nine?"

I loved spending time with my dad but I was undecided. I knew I was going to crush him on the links but these times together came fewer than wanted.

"Sure. But I'm pretty good," I said.

"Ok," he chuckled as he loaded my clubs in the trunk and we headed off.

On the first tee, he took honors and striped a long drive right down the middle of the fairway.

Lucky shot, I thought, as I drove, my ball landing twenty yards behind his.

His luck continued throughout the round. Every drive of his landed in the fairway, each wedge nestled close to the pin, and his putting was pure. I played well enough but in the end he beat me by twelve strokes, and we only played nine holes.

"Dad, how? How did you play so well? I've watched you for years and you lost every round you played. Have you been taking lessons?" I asked.

He chuckled, then spoke. "Mark, you confuse losing with proficiency. You always asked if I won and I answered honestly, no. But you never asked if I signed a new client or gained additional business after the round. To the later question, I always did. When I first started out selling and had golf meetings, I would win, and by a lot. Each potential customer was embarrassed and angry and stormed off the course without even discussing potential business. I soon learned that, when my opponent was winning, he was happier and more willing to discuss business terms. From that moment I changed the way I thought about the game. I didn't consider the time as a competition but more as an opportunity to create a relationship. That's when I started to see my sales increase."

A Junior's Match

"JOE! COME HERE. That's not acceptable behavior on the golf course."

"Whatever," Joe said then turned and walked back towards the green.

A few holes later, Joe once again showed poor conduct as he hit out of turn but, more importantly, didn't announce his intention to play nor confirm the area was clear and nearly hit his competitor during his backswing.

"Joe! As your coach, I'm telling you if you continue those actions, I will contact a marshal. I don't care that you're winning your match or that our team will lose the championship or that there will be no trophy for the school to display. Integrity is more important than winning."

"You wouldn't dare," Joe said, staring at his coach.

"I would. Be sure of that," Coach Miller stated, firmly.

Without acknowledging the comment, Joe returned to his match. Unfortunately, a few holes later, Joe again nearly struck his opponent.

"Marshal," Coach Miller called out, to which the marshal came near, followed by Joe who was taken aback at the follow through on the threat from his coach.

"My player is being reckless and endangering other players. You need to warn him and, if he doesn't conform, you need to disqualify him."

"I have noticed the behavior and it is unacceptable. I also noticed you warning your player and was hoping his actions would change but that obviously did not happen," the marshal spoke.

Turning to Joe, the marshal continued. "This is your official warning that, if you endanger another competitor or a spectator through the rest of your round, I'll be forced to disqualify you. Do you understand?"

"Yes," Joe mumbled.

"Good," the marshal responded. "Continue your match."

A few holes later, the marshal approached Coach Miller. "I've witnessed another blatant breach in etiquette and, for the safety of players and spectators, I'm disqualifying your player and expelling him from the course."

"Understood," Coach Miller replied.

"No way!" Joe pleaded. "I'm winning."

"Sorry, son, I hope you learn from this," the marshal said.

"Head to the clubhouse," Coach Miller directed. "I'll see you when the rest of the matches are complete."

After the round, Coach Miller collected Joe and left the course. For some time, there was nothing but quiet from both riders until Joe spoke.

"Mom is going to be so mad at you, Dad."

"And you, too, Joe."

The Heir to Golf

"HELLO?"

"Greetings. Am I speaking with Diana?"

"Yes. Who is this?"

"This is Richard Todd, calling from Edinburgh, in Scotland, on behalf of the Royal and Ancient Golf Club."

"Really? I don't know anyone from Scotland. What do you want?"

"I have been charged with the task of finding relatives of an individual."

"I don't have any money, if that's what you're getting at."

"No, no. I can assure you I am not asking for money nor is this some type of scam. My research shows your ancestors may have come from Scotland. Does the name Rattray sound familiar?"

"Yes. My great-grandma's maiden name was Rattray. Why do you ask?"

"It appears your great-great-great-great uncle was Captain of The Golf."

"Was that a military title?"

"No, ma'am. He was the winner of the first golf tournament held in Leith by the Gentleman Golfers of Edinburgh, later becoming the Honorable Company of Edinburgh Golfers. As you may know, the 300th anniversary of that match is approaching and my research has found that you are the last relative of Captain Rattray. Would you be inclined to accept, on his behalf, a recognition for his accomplishments?"

"Would that recognition be a large sum of money?"

"No. It's strictly an honorary mention."

"Like I said, I don't have any money, especially to pay for a trip to Scotland."

"Ma'am, all expenses for you and your family to attend would be covered by the R&A."

"When do we leave?"

"Brilliant. I'll mail you an itinerary and all the necessary information. I'm thrilled you are willing to partake in the ceremony. Thank you and goodbye."

"Goodbye," Diana said as she hung up the phone.

"Who was that?" her husband questioned.

"You'll never believe it …"

Months later, in Scotland

"Welcome, everyone, to St. Andrew. We are here to celebrate the Honorable Men of Leith, who had the first official golf match and laid down the original 13 rules of golf. That day was the birth of the current modern game we all love. And the winner of that first match was none other than Mister Rattray. And here today, to help us honor him, is none other than his own descendant. Welcome, onto the stage, Diana Rattray-Smith!"

"Diana. I understand it is your first trip to this sacred land. What are your thoughts of our hallowed grounds?" the emcee spoke.

"The area is quite amazing. I'm really in awe of the sprawling and rolling lands with its beautiful agricultural and architecture," Diana responded, followed by cheers from the crowd.

"Brilliant. Thank you very much. Without further delay, let the 300th match at St. Andrew's commence. And to bestow the highest honor to the family of Rattray, let his relative put a ceremony ball into play. Diana, please enter the teeing area for the opening drive," the emcee announced.

Um," Diana mumbled, then spoke to the crowd. "I would be most honored, but I'm not a golfer."

The Caddy's Tip

I WAS A CADDY when I was in high school at the local country club. I was very fortunate to have that job as the pay was good, but it was a lot of work.

As a caddy, if you were lucky, you would pull a double bag and squeeze in two rounds on any given day. That meant four tips! Sure it meant running twice as hard but, when you're a teenager and trying to fill your gas tank and have money for dates, you are willing to do about anything.

And anything included being yelled at for not finding someone's ball that went into the pond, talked down to because your knowledge of the rules were different from theirs (that doesn't mean I was wrong), scolded because you couldn't keep up with their pace (Really? You were in a motorized cart and I was carrying two bags and still only ten yards behind you!), frowned at because your drive went out of bounds – twice on the same hole – cursed at because the cart girl wasn't there when someone was thirsty, and belittled for not finding your forest-bound ball faster. Of the latter, I spent more time in the woods than a deer. I had poison ivy all summer long.

I guess some of the other caddies didn't want the money as bad as I did for several of them were always in the caddy shack, or only would loop once a day and never carry a double. Fine by me, as that gave me extra opportunity.

What really irked me was the kid that did nothing other than clean golf clubs when each golfer finished. Really, that was a position. You sat around for hours until someone finished a loop, spent five minutes per bag cleaning the clubs, maybe wipe down the outside of the golf bag if the owner had a dirty round, and go back to reading your comic book. That's all the job entailed.

I always thought that kid was terribly lazy but never gave him a piece of my mind until the end of that summer. On the last day the course was open, after I collected my final tip, I went to talk to him.

"Hey, what gives? Are you just lazy or what?" I said.

"I'm not lazy, just smart," he replied.

"How do you figure?" I responded.

"I see you working hard, pulling doubles and working from sunrise to sunset. Good for you. But let me ask, how much do you earn in tips?"

"I generally get five bucks per bag. If I double carry then that's ten and if I loop twice twenty goes in my pocket," I said proudly.

"That's not bad. You definitely earned that money. You look pretty exhausted at the end of most days. I, on the other hand, see about forty bags a day. At least half of those people stiff me, the other half give me a dollar or two each. So, on a normal day, I bring home close to forty dollars. All that money for a combined couple hours of minimal effort. So, I'll answer your question. Yup, I'm lazy, and I'm smart, and I earned twice as much as you for less than half the work. See ya next summer, dummy."

That season I learned a valuable lesson: hard work is great but smart work is better. I also recall that experience every time I have my clubs cleaned after a round. I always tip low, but something, and raise an eyebrow and check the kid out.

Keep this story in mind when you tip your caddy, the person that was at your side for four hours, carrying a heavy bag, helping you track and find your shots, and ready to provide helpful information.

The Grave Hole

PETE WAS A FARMER, seventh generation. He loved his land and was proud of the crops he grew on his two hundred acres.

Over the years Pete's neighbors, who were also farmers, eventually retired and sold their properties. These once thriving agricultural grounds soon became housing sub-developments, strip malls, and parking lots.

One of the nearby businesses was a golf course, a very prosperous and upscale track. The owner was always looking to expand, desiring another eighteen holes along with some homes, banquette hall, or practice area.

"I will not sell to you," Pete would say after every frequent request by Mr. Green of Sugar Bush Golf Links, to buy his land. "I plan to be buried on the land I love."

Years passed and, as happens, Pete eventually died.

Soon thereafter, the local priest and Mr. Green were called to the courthouse for the reading of Pete's will.

Well, there's only two of us here. Maybe the old geezer decided to give me the land, Mr. Green thought as he sat in the private chambers of the judge in front of an old oak desk.

"Thank you for coming. This is a rather unusual case and, having known Pete all my life, I decided to handle it personally," the judge spoke. "I will read the Last Will and Testament of Pete Herman along with comments he included: 'As stated many times before, I wish to be buried on the property that I worked daily for over seventy-five years and that my parents, their parents, their parents, their parents, their parents, and their parents worked also.'"

Seriously? That mean old goat called me in here just to rub it in my face one more time, Mr. Green considered.

"'Therefore, I request Father Padre to make sure my request happens and it is done with all the pomp and circumstance that he can muster. I wish to be laid to rest near the large oak tree, in the shade, toward the back of my property.'"

"So shall it be done," Father Padre spoke into the air.

"And where's that leave me?" Mr. Green asked.

"I'm not finished," the judge responded curtly, taking a little longer to continue than normal.

"'The remaining one-hundred-ninety-nine and two-thirds acres are to be donated to Sugar Bush Golf Links with the understanding that my grave site is to be marked as out of bounds. I also wish to be invited yearly to their tournament, although I may be unable to attend.'"

"Any questions?" the judge asked looking back and forth between the two men sitting in from of him. "Good. Thank you for coming in. You will receive documents from the courts providing legal statements to represent this will. Please see yourself out as I have a tee time this afternoon and I'm running late."

~

Years later, Sugar Bush Golf Links finished the addition of another eighteen holes. And, as directed, Pete's gravesite was marked out of bounds. Even more so, a small grove of trees was planted around his tomb, which protected it from stray balls and wandering golfers from the thirteenth hole, named The Grave Hole. A small, lightly-tread path lead from the thirteenth fairway to his gravestone, which was in the shape of a bench. Yearly, an envelope with the return address of Sugar Bush Golf Links could be seen under the seat.

Other titles from The Golf Rules…

The Golf Rules

Learn the rules of golf by watching others break them,

a humorous story focusing on stroke play format.

The Golf Rules-Etiquette

Enhance your golf etiquette by watching others' mistakes,

follow a municipal golfer on a country club course.

And more *Short Stories from the Long Links*!

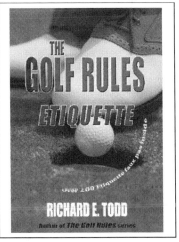

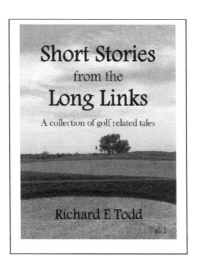

I'd love your feedback! Please post a <u>review</u> on Amazon.

Follow TGR on
Facebook, Twitter, WordPress, YouTube,
and on our website.

www.**TheGolfRules**.com

Made in the USA
Columbia, SC
29 December 2017